REASONABLE: A NEW WAY OF BEING

By C. J. Sand

"You never change things by fighting the existing reality. To change something, build a new model that makes the existing model obsolete."

Buckminster Fuller

C. J. Sand

"There isn't anything new in this book. These common sense, humane ideas have been around for centuries. I've simply taken these ideas and given them a form, a direction, an elegance, and a name ..."

C. J. Sand

Reasonable

adjective: rea-son-able

Definition: fair and sensible

Synonyms – equitable, fair, honest, humane, impartial, objective, rational, sensible, understandable.

Antonyms – biased, irrational, partial, prejudiced, unfair, unjust, incomprehensible.

R

Welcome to Reasonable

Reasonable is a positive alternative to atheism.

With Reasonable there is no supreme being to worship, no mythology to believe in and no faith is necessary.

With Reasonable there are no promises of heaven or threats of hell.

With Reasonable the emphasis is on finding harmony, balance and happiness in your life while treating yourself and others as you would like to be treated.

With Reasonable there are no long lists of laws to obey, no thick, confusing books to read and no obligatory services to attend.

Reasonable is designed to be 'elegant', in the scientific sense. To be 'breathtakingly simple'. In fact, everything you need to know about Reasonable is contained in this small book.

How Does One Become 'Reasonable'?

To become 'Reasonable' all one needs to do is to accept the Reasonable Beliefs and use the Reasonable Guidelines to help live and enjoy their lives.

To find out more, please visit our website at:

iamreasonable.com

The Symbol for Our Movement

The symbol for Reasonable is a capital letter R. Elegant, just like our beliefs.

Why Not Just Be an Atheist?

Good question. Why not just be an atheist? But names matter. Names matter a lot. Atheists are referred to, or refer to themselves, in the negative. A-theist, one who is without a god. How many other movements or beliefs refer to themselves this way? When one meets a Christian do they introduce themselves as an 'Anti-Satanist'? Of course not. Would a Muslim refer to themselves as 'Non-Kafir'? I doubt it. Would a Jew introduce themselves as 'Agentile'? Never in a million years. And yet, Atheists cannot shake the whole 'god' thing, because it's right there in the name.
People who do not believe in a god can also be given other, less than desirable, labels such as 'Nonbeliever', 'Non Religous', 'Pagan' and 'Nones' (as in 'none of the above' when filling out a form). We find this to be unacceptable.

We refer to ourselves as 'Reasonable' because it is what we are, not what we are not.

The Stigma Associated with Atheism

We feel that there is a negative stigma in our culture attached to the label of 'Atheist'. Because Atheists don't believe in a god, then many assume that they don't believe in anything, are prone to criminal activity and are not to be trusted. The image of a disheveled, bitter communist sitting in a darkened room with a bottle of vodka in one hand and a pistol in the other comes to mind. References to Mao Zedong, Pol Pot and Joseph Stalin are common. We want to distance ourselves from these perceptions. Reasonable is a liberating, enlightening and uplifting movement that has nothing to do with these negative stereotypes.

Arguing with People of Faith

It seems as if many atheists and humanists spend an inordinate amount of their time debating, arguing with and belittling people of faith. We do not agree with this strategy. We feel that if people choose to believe in something, and it gives value and meaning to their lives, then that's their business and none of ours. We choose to live and let live. We choose not to take part in criticizing or belittling people of faith. That being said, we will stand up for our rights when politicians try to make one person's 'religious belief' into our 'law'.

Power Corrupts

Because this is true, Reasonable will never be a 'religion' in the conventional sense. There will be no clergy, no churches and no heirarchy of any kind. It does not need them. The elegant beliefs and guide-lines spelled out in this book stand on their own and don't need professional interpretation.

If like-minded people want to get together to share and discuss these ideas, then they are free to do so in a park, a restaurant, a coffee shop, online or in the priv-acy of their own homes.

An Emphasis on Individuality and Equality

At Reasonable, we understand that some human beings are born with special gifts, talents and aptitudes that can be of value to themselves and to our world. That being said, Reasonable does not accept the premise that any one race, noble lineage or aristocratic bloodline has more of these virtues than any other. We believe that we are all unique, talented individuals and members of one race, the human race. Our challenge is to create an environment here on Earth where everyone is given the opportunity to use whatever abilities they may possess to make our world a better place for everyone.

The Reasonable Beliefs

1. Let go of mythology, superstition and fear.

2. Treat yourself and the world you live in as you would like to be treated, with love, generosity, honesty and respect.

3. Being reasonable consists of the right to do whatever does not infringe on the rights of others: thus, exercise of these rights has no limits other than those which secure to other members of society enjoyment of those same rights.

4. The point of life is to be happy. Strive to find your happiness in living a balanced, harmonic, and loving life.

5. Reasonable is gender, age, racial, ethnic and sexual orientation neutral.

The Reasonable Guidelines

1. In all things, strive to do no harm.

2. Work for balance and harmony in all things. Avoid extremism in any form.

3. Take responsibility for your own choices and actions.

4. Do things because you choose to do them, not because you are made to do them.

5. Question everything. Test all things against the facts. Be ready to let go of familiar, traditional or comfortable beliefs if they do not stand up to the evidence.

6. Let go of the pain from the past. Forgive others, but forgive yourself first.

7. Always seek to be learning or creating something new.

8. Work and play with the same interest and enthusiasm. Make it difficult for others to see any difference between the two.

9. Within your power, speak out against injustice, discrimination and tyranny in your world.

10. If you make a mess, clean it up.

11. Be wary of any person or institution that attempts to frighten you, inflames your passions or tries to take advantage of your sense of duty.

12. Be wary of any person or institution that insists upon unquestioned belief, loyalty, and obedience.

13. To the best of your ability, only speak the truth.

R

Inspiring Quotes

"Complexity is your enemy. Any fool can make something complicated. It is hard to make something simple."

Richard Branson

"Liberty consists in the right to do whatever is not contrary to the rights of others: thus, exercise of the natural rights of each individual has no limits other than those which secure to other members of society enjoyment of the same rights."

Thomas Paine

"It's the same each time with progress. First they ignore you, then they say you're mad, then dangerous, then there's a pause and then you can't find anyone who disagrees with you."

Tony Benn

R

"When I was 5 years old, my mother always told me that happiness was the key to life. When I went to school, they asked me what I wanted to be when I grew up. I wrote down 'happy'. They told me I didn't understand the assignment, and I told them they didn't understand life."

John Lennon

"How can we be focused on a higher level of existence when we spend so much time looking for faults in others?"

Unknown

"The secret of change is to focus all your energy, not on fighting the old, but on building the new."

Dan Millman

C. J. Sand

"Men occasionally stumble over the truth, but most of them pick themselves up and hurry off as if nothing ever happened."

Winston Churchill

"Define yourself by what you love. Be pro-stuff, not just anti-stuff."

Tim Minchin

*"Time is given us to be happy and for no other reason . . .
when we waste time, we waste happiness."*

L. Frank Baum

Printed in Great Britain
by Amazon